Foreign Lawyers in Indonesia: Between Global Collaboration and Legal Sovereignty

Muhammad Ari Pratomo

Published by PT MuhammadAriLaw Pustaka Nada, 2025.

Foreign Lawyers in Indonesia Between Global Collaboration and Legal Sovereignty

Muhammad Ari Pratomo

Also by Muhammad Ari Pratomo

LEGAL MECHANISMS OF FOREIGN INVESTMENT iN NDONESIA
The Daily Pen of a Lawyer
Foreign Lawyers in Indonesia: Between Global Collaboration and Legal Sovereignty
The Final Judgement
Youth at the End of Time – A Guide to a Broken World
Back to Father's Embrace

Watch for more at https://muhammadarilaw.com.

To every Indonesian lawyerwho stands firmfor justice, professionalism,and the sovereignty of our legal systemin the face of global pressure.

And to the silenced voices—may the law speak for youwhen no one else will.

— Muhammad Ari Pratomo

"Justice must travel, but sovereignty must never vanish in transit."— Muhammad Ari Pratomo

Foreign Lawyers in Indonesia

Between Global Collaboration and Legal Sovereignty

Description:

Foreign Lawyers in Indonesia: Between Global Collaboration and Legal Sovereignty is a timely and essential exploration of how Indonesia regulates the presence and role of foreign lawyers within its national legal framework. Written by Indonesian lawyer, author, and legal communicator Muhammad Ari Pratomo, this book provides a clear and comprehensive overview of the legal boundaries, licensing requirements, and ethical limitations for foreign legal practitioners operating in Indonesia.

Combining sharp legal analysis with real-world insights, this book navigates the intersection of international cooperation and national sovereignty. It is a vital reference for legal scholars, policy makers, law firms, and global professionals who seek to understand Indonesia's position in a rapidly evolving legal landscape.

Whether you're a foreign legal consultant, a local practitioner, or a student of international law, this book offers clarity in a complex field—amplifying the voice of legal sovereignty in a globally connected era.

Foreword

In an increasingly interconnected legal world, the role and limitations of foreign lawyers have become more relevant than ever—especially in a country like Indonesia, where the tension between globalization and legal sovereignty is tangible. This book was born out of my experience and concern as a legal practitioner navigating these evolving dynamics.

It is no longer uncommon to see global law firms seeking entry into Indonesia or multinational clients looking for cross-border legal services. But how far does Indonesian law permit foreign lawyers to operate? And to what extent must those boundaries be maintained to protect our legal system and support local practitioners?

This book is intended as both a practical legal guide and a reflective analysis of the current regulatory landscape. I have outlined the legal basis, licensing procedures, role limitations, and ethical considerations governing the presence of foreign lawyers in Indonesia. My aim is to strike a balanced perspective—that global collaboration need not undermine sovereignty, and that protecting local advocates does not mean closing the door to international legal knowledge.

I hope this book serves not only as a reference but also as a thoughtful contribution to the ongoing legal discourse in Indonesia and beyond. Whether you are a student, academic, policymaker, or legal professional, I believe this work will offer clarity in a complex field.

Finally, I extend my deepest gratitude to everyone who supported the writing of this book. May this humble contribution serve the legal community with purpose and integrity.

Warm regards,

Muhammad Ari Pratomo

Author & Indonesian Lawyer

Table of Contents

Introduction

Why This Topic Matters

In the age of globalization and open legal markets, the practice of law is no longer confined to national borders. Multinational corporations, foreign investors, and transnational clients increasingly require legal services that can navigate multiple legal systems. Meanwhile, countries like Indonesia remain committed to the principle of legal sovereignty as a fundamental pillar in preserving their national legal identity and judicial integrity.

The presence of foreign lawyers or foreign legal consultants in Indonesia represents a point of intersection—and at times, tension—between two major forces: global collaboration and national legal sovereignty. This is precisely where the urgency of this topic lies.

Purpose of This Book

This book aims to provide a comprehensive, accurate, and legally grounded understanding of:

- Who qualifies as a foreign lawyer or foreign legal consultant in Indonesia?
- What legal frameworks govern their presence and activities?
- What requirements, restrictions, and permissions exist under Indonesian law?
- How does Indonesia's approach compare to other jurisdictions?
- What are the future challenges and policy recommendations for maintaining legal openness while protecting national interests?

Methodology and Sources

This book adopts a normative-legal approach, referencing:

- Law No. 18 of 2003 on Advocates
- Government Regulation No. 2 of 2008
- Ministry of Law and Human Rights Regulation No. 26 of 2017
- National and international legal literature
- Comparative studies from ASEAN and common law countries
- The author's personal experience in handling cross-border legal matters

The content is crafted to be accessible to a wide audience, including law students, junior advocates, academics, legal bureaucrats, and domestic law firms engaged with foreign entities.

Legal Framework in Indonesia

Advocates Law & PERADI

Indonesia's legal profession is regulated through a unified framework that draws its authority primarily from **Law No. 18 of 2003 on Advocates** (***Undang-Undang Nomor 18 Tahun 2003 tentang Advokat***). This law establishes the status, rights, obligations, and ethical standards of advocates practicing in Indonesia, and it serves as the core legal reference for understanding how legal services must operate within the country's jurisdiction.

Definition of an Advocate

According to Article 1(1) of the Advocates Law, an **Advocate** is defined as someone whose profession is to provide legal services, both inside and outside court, who meets the legal requirements and is authorized under the law. This includes roles such as legal consultants, defense counsel, legal advisors, and other professional roles tied to legal service provision.

The law stipulates that the title and role of "Advocate" are reserved **only for Indonesian citizens** who have undergone advocate training, passed the national bar exam, completed an internship, and been officially sworn in by the High Court.

Thus, **foreign nationals are prohibited** from holding the title of "Advocate" under Indonesian law, regardless of their qualifications in their home countries.

The Role of PERADI

PERADI (***Perhimpunan Advokat Indonesia*** or Indonesian Advocates Association) is the **only professional organization** recognized by the law to regulate, license, and oversee Indonesian advocates. Its functions include:

- Administering bar exams
- Providing professional ethics and discipline oversight
- Handling certification and registration
- Representing the advocate profession nationally and internationally

PERADI operates under the mandate of the Advocates Law and works closely with the Supreme Court and the Ministry of Law and Human Rights. Any legal professional practicing law in Indonesia must either be a registered PERADI advocate or clearly fall outside the restricted roles—such as in-house counsel or certain governmental legal functions.

Implications for Foreign Lawyers

Given this legal framework, **foreign lawyers are not allowed to practice independently** as advocates in Indonesia. They may, however, **serve as foreign legal consultants** under strict regulatory supervision and only in specific advisory roles.

This distinction is essential: a foreign national cannot act as legal counsel in court, represent clients in litigation, or engage in legal advocacy involving Indonesian law unless specifically permitted under a narrow exception, which is often tied to bilateral agreements or government approval.

Foreign Legal Consultants

Key Regulations & Definitions

Indonesia acknowledges the increasing need for cross-border legal expertise, particularly in areas of international trade, investment law, and multinational business operations. However, the legal system has established **strict and well-defined parameters** for foreign lawyers through the designation of **Foreign Legal Consultants (FLCs)**.

Definition and Legal Status

Under **Ministry of Law and Human Rights Regulation No. 26 of 2017** on Requirements and Procedures for the Employment of Foreign Advocates as Foreign Legal Consultants, a **Foreign Legal Consultant (FLC)** is defined as:

"A foreign national who holds qualifications and professional licenses in his or her country of origin to provide legal services, and who is granted a temporary permit to advise on international law or the law of the country where they are qualified, without practicing Indonesian law."

The key limitation is clear: **FLCs are not permitted to practice or represent clients in Indonesian law**. Their services are strictly **limited to advisory roles** on the law of their country of origin or international legal matters.

Legal Basis

The role and scope of FLCs in Indonesia are primarily governed by:

- **Law No. 18 of 2003 on Advocates**
- **Government Regulation No. 2 of 2008** on the Use of Foreign Advocates
- **Ministerial Regulation No. 26 of 2017**
- Guidelines issued by **PERADI** and related institutions

Scope of Advisory Practice

A registered FLC may:

- Provide legal advice on the law of his/her country of origin
- Advise on international business transactions
- Work in partnership with Indonesian law firms in a **non-litigation** capacity
- Assist in **cross-border deals or arbitration** that involve jurisdictions outside Indonesia

An FLC may **not**:

- Represent clients in Indonesian courts
- Draft or sign documents governed by Indonesian law
- Deliver legal opinions that pertain to Indonesian law
- Engage in pro bono litigation or dispute resolution under Indonesian jurisdiction

Duration and Licensing

Licensing for an FLC is:

- **Temporary and renewable**

- Issued by the **Ministry of Law and Human Rights**
- Subject to **annual review** and conditional upon the FLC being employed by a **registered Indonesian law firm**

The FLC must also:

- Have a **minimum of five years' experience**
- Pass **fit and proper evaluations**
- Comply with reporting and ethical obligations
- Conduct **legal knowledge transfer programs** to benefit local lawyers (a key requirement for knowledge exchange)

Requirements & Licensing

Permits, Firm Affiliation, and Restrictions

While Indonesia permits the limited participation of foreign lawyers in the legal sector, it does so under **strict administrative and ethical requirements**. Becoming a **Foreign Legal Consultant (FLC)** in Indonesia involves a regulated licensing process, firm affiliation, and professional restrictions that are essential to understand before engaging in any form of legal advisory work in the country.

Licensing Authority

The main authority for granting FLC permits is the **Ministry of Law and Human Rights of the Republic of Indonesia**, specifically through the **Directorate General of Legal Administration.**

Licensing is **not automatic** and must be applied for individually. The application must be endorsed by a registered Indonesian law firm willing to employ the foreign lawyer under Indonesian jurisdiction.

Minimum Requirements

To be eligible for a license as a Foreign Legal Consultant in Indonesia, the applicant must:

- **Be a foreign national** with legal qualifications in their home country
- Have **at least 5 years of experience** practicing law after qualification
- **Not have been sanctioned** or disbarred in their country of origin
- Submit proof of education, licensing, and a **certificate of good standing**

- Be sponsored by an **Indonesian law firm**, which will act as the host institution
- Provide a **detailed work plan**, including how they will contribute to the legal sector through knowledge-sharing or capacity - building programs

Firm Affiliation

A foreign legal consultant **must be affiliated** with an Indonesian law firm that has been registered and recognized by the Ministry. The firm:

- Bears **joint responsibility** for the conduct of the foreign lawyer
- Must ensure that the FLC does not engage in prohibited legal practice
- Must provide opportunities for **legal knowledge transfer**, in the form of training sessions, workshops, or mentoring programs for Indonesian advocates
- Must submit annual reports about the FLC's activities

Validity and Renewal

- The permit is **valid for one year** and may be **renewed annually**
- The FLC must maintain continuous compliance with Indonesian regulations
- Any violation, such as practicing Indonesian law or litigation, may lead to **revocation of the permit** and legal sanctions

Core Restrictions

Even with a valid license, FLCs **cannot**:

- Represent clients in court (litigation is strictly prohibited)
- Draft or sign legal documents governed by Indonesian law
- Use the title "Advocate" in any formal or informal capacity

- Establish their own law firm or practice independently in Indonesia
- Give legal opinions related to Indonesian statutory or case law

They **can**:

- Provide consultation on **foreign law** or **international legal matters**
- Advise on **cross-border transactions**
- Work in collaboration with their Indonesian host firm for **non-litigation projects**

This chapter emphasizes that Indonesia welcomes foreign expertise under **controlled and respectful terms**, ensuring that the national legal identity and the role of local advocates remain protected.

Scope of Practice & Limitations

What Foreign Lawyers Can and Cannot Do

Foreign legal professionals working in Indonesia under the title of **Foreign Legal Consultant (FLC)** must adhere to a well-defined and **strictly limited scope of practice**. These limitations are not merely administrative but are deeply rooted in the principle of **legal sovereignty**, ensuring that the legal profession within Indonesia remains in the hands of qualified Indonesian citizens.

Permitted Activities

Foreign Legal Consultants are allowed to:

- **Advise on the law of their home country** or any other foreign jurisdiction in which they are licensed

- Provide **consultation on international legal matters**, including international commercial contracts, mergers and acquisitions, trade compliance, and arbitration
- Collaborate with Indonesian advocates in **non-litigation legal services**, such as due diligence, contract review (excluding those governed by Indonesian law), or advisory roles in cross-border transactions
- Conduct **internal training, workshops, and capacity-building programs** for Indonesian lawyers within their affiliated law firms
- Serve as **strategic advisors** for multinational corporations or foreign investors operating in Indonesia, provided they do not cross into areas reserved for Indonesian advocates

Prohibited Activities

Foreign Legal Consultants are **strictly prohibited** from:

- **Practicing Indonesian law** in any capacity, including providing opinions or legal advice on Indonesian statutes or court decisions
- **Representing clients in Indonesian courts or before government agencies**, whether in civil, criminal, administrative, or religious matters
- **Signing or drafting legal documents** governed by Indonesian law (e.g., land deeds, notarial acts, litigation pleadings)
- Using the professional title of "**Advocate**" in Indonesia or misleading the public to believe they are authorized to fully practice law
- **Establishing an independent law firm** or acting as a principal in a legal entity offering Indonesian legal services

- Engaging in **pro bono litigation**, public interest advocacy, or dispute resolution involving Indonesian law

Ethical Obligations

Even within their limited scope, FLCs must uphold the highest standards of:

- **Confidentiality and client privilege**
- **Professional responsibility** under both Indonesian regulations and the ethical code of their home jurisdiction
- **Transparency in public communication**, including marketing and firm representation
- **Non-competition** with local lawyers in areas restricted by law
- **Compliance** with all permit conditions, including reporting duties to the Ministry and participation in legal knowledge transfer

Penalties for Non-Compliance

Violating these limitations can result in:

- **Immediate revocation** of the FLC permit
- **Legal sanctions**, including fines and deportation
- **Blacklisting from future practice** in Indonesia
- **Sanctions for the host Indonesian law firm**, including suspension of licenses or registration

This framework reflects Indonesia's approach to balancing **openness to global legal talent** while **safeguarding its legal jurisdiction**. Foreign legal consultants are welcomed as **collaborators**, not as substitutes for Indonesian advocates.

Comparative Global Practices

ASEAN & International Case Studies

The regulation of foreign lawyers is not unique to Indonesia. Across the world—particularly in **ASEAN countries and major global legal hubs**—there exists a diverse range of approaches in determining how, when, and to what extent foreign legal professionals may operate within national borders.

This chapter explores **comparative models** from selected jurisdictions to provide a clearer view of global norms, best practices, and the uniqueness of the Indonesian framework.

Singapore: Controlled Liberalization

Singapore is often cited as a model of **legal market openness with control**. Foreign law practices are allowed through:

- **Foreign Law Practice** (**FLP**) licenses
- **Joint Law Ventures** (**JLV**) with local firms
- **Qualifying Foreign Law Practice** (**QFLP**) schemes

Foreign lawyers in Singapore may practice foreign law and certain aspects of Singapore law (mainly commercial), but full rights of audience in court remain reserved for **Singapore-qualified advocates**.

Key Insight: Singapore balances its status as a global financial hub with strict protection of litigation and domestic legal integrity.

Malaysia: National Sovereignty First

Malaysia maintains a **highly protective** stance. While foreign lawyers can advise on **foreign law**, they are strictly prohibited from engaging in local legal matters. Licenses are granted only with heavy conditions, and participation in litigation or any domestic legal practice is forbidden.

Key Insight: Malaysia's approach is closest to Indonesia's, with strong emphasis on **legal sovereignty and preservation of national practice**.

Thailand: Foreign Law Only

Thailand allows foreign lawyers to register and provide **foreign legal services**, but does **not permit practice of Thai law**, court representation, or law firm ownership. All legal opinions on Thai law must be issued by licensed Thai lawyers.

Key Insight: Similar to Indonesia, Thailand makes a clear line between **advisory foreign counsel** and **domestic legal authority**.

United States & United Kingdom: Mutual Recognition

In contrast, jurisdictions like the **U.S.** and **U.K.** follow **liberal recognition schemes**:

- In the **U.S.**, each state determines its rules; some allow foreign lawyers to take the bar (e.g., New York, California) under specific conditions.
- The **U.K.** allows registration as a **Registered Foreign Lawyer (RFL)** and **Qualified Lawyers Transfer Scheme (QLTS)** (now replaced by **SQE**), which enables foreign lawyers to requalify and practice fully.

Key Insight: These systems are designed to **integrate foreign lawyers**, reflecting their common law traditions and global legal market focus.

Japan & South Korea: Structured Pathways

Both countries offer limited licenses for foreign lawyers under **Registered Foreign Lawyer** schemes. These licenses come with stringent experience requirements and **restrictions on practicing local law**.

However, Japan and Korea encourage **knowledge transfer** and **collaboration** with local firms—much like Indonesia's model.

Lessons for Indonesia

Indonesia's legal framework aligns with most ASEAN nations in:

- **Prohibiting foreign lawyers from practicing local law**
- **Requiring firm affiliation** and supervised licensing
- **Emphasizing knowledge-sharing as a condition**

However, Indonesia can improve by:

- Providing more **transparent application procedures**
- Encouraging **joint training initiatives**
- Expanding legal infrastructure to facilitate **cross-border collaboration** without compromising sovereignty

This comparative overview reveals that **Indonesia is not isolated** in its restrictions, but rather, follows a cautious and sovereignty-based model shared across many jurisdictions. The global trend suggests **calibrated openness**, and Indonesia is well-positioned to evolve its policy while remaining true to its legal identity.

Legal Globalization vs. Sovereignty

Challenges and Opportunities

In an increasingly interconnected world, legal systems are not immune to globalization. **Cross-border transactions, international arbitration, digital trade**, and **transnational legal disputes** have all created a demand for collaboration among legal professionals of various nationalities. However, this rising trend often clashes with one fundamental principle: **national legal sovereignty**.

Indonesia, like many countries, faces the ongoing dilemma: **How do we open our legal market to global players while preserving the integrity and independence of our domestic legal system?**

The Promise of Legal Globalization

Legal globalization offers multiple benefits:

- **Increased foreign investment** through legal certainty in cross-border transactions
- **Capacity-building** through exposure to global best practices
- Access to **specialized legal expertise** in fields such as international trade, competition law, maritime law, and intellectual property
- Opportunities for **professional exchange programs**, law firm partnerships, and co-counsel arrangements
- Enhancement of **Indonesia's international arbitration competitiveness**

These outcomes could elevate the Indonesian legal ecosystem if carefully integrated.

The Risks to Sovereignty

However, unregulated foreign participation in legal services poses serious risks:

- **Dilution of national legal identity**, especially if foreign counsel begins to dominate complex litigation or high-profile commercial cases
- **Loss of advocacy space** for local lawyers, potentially marginalizing Indonesian legal professionals
- **Ethical conflicts** due to different standards of practice and client obligations
- **Security and confidentiality risks** in sensitive state-related cases involving foreign legal entities
- Erosion of **local legal traditions and indigenous jurisprudence**

Indonesia must remain vigilant in protecting its legal sovereignty while engaging globally.

Striking the Balance

To balance globalization and sovereignty, a hybrid model is crucial. This means:

- Permitting **foreign involvement only in defined areas**, such as foreign law advisory or joint international matters
- **Prohibiting litigation** or any representation in domestic courts by foreign lawyers
- Requiring **local firm affiliation** to ensure accountability and mutual knowledge sharing
- Emphasizing **legal transfer programs**, mentorship, and collaborative training as conditions for licensing

- Creating **clear regulatory pathways** for foreign legal professionals, including ethical codes aligned with national standards

Policy Recommendations

Indonesia should consider:

- **Codifying comprehensive FLC laws** beyond ministerial regulations
- Enhancing **transparency and accessibility** in permit procedures
- Encouraging **bilateral legal cooperation agreements** with strategic countries
- Creating a **registry of FLCs** accessible to the public and the Bar
- Promoting **cross-border legal research and academic collaboration**

Such policies will help Indonesia participate in the global legal community while asserting its **judicial independence** and **professional integrity**.

Recommendations for the Future

As Indonesia continues to grow into a regional economic powerhouse, the country's legal system must adapt to balance national interests with global engagement. This chapter outlines actionable **policy directions and reform strategies** to refine the presence and role of foreign lawyers in Indonesia—ensuring both **regulatory clarity** and **professional synergy** without undermining sovereignty.

Codification of Foreign Legal Consultant (FLC) Rules

Currently, the framework for foreign lawyers in Indonesia is regulated mainly through ministerial regulations and guidelines. For stronger legal certainty:

- A dedicated **chapter in the Advocates Law** or a stand-alone **Foreign Legal Services Law** should be created.
- This law should define FLC status, licensing procedures, scope of practice, disciplinary measures, and sunset clauses.
- Regulatory authority should be **clearly delegated**, ideally to a single oversight body with coordination from PERADI and the Ministry of Law and Human Rights.

Centralized and Transparent Licensing Mechanism

To streamline foreign lawyer entry while preventing abuse:

- A **single online platform** should handle FLC applications, renewals, and monitoring.
- Application criteria must be **published transparently**, including mandatory legal experience, local firm affiliation, and ethical declarations.

- A **national FLC registry** should be made public for clients and firms to verify credentials.

Strengthening Legal Collaboration Without Undermining Local Practice

Reforms should focus on collaboration, not competition:

- Require FLCs to conduct **mandatory legal education or training** sessions for Indonesian advocates each year.
- Establish **co-counseling protocols** for international arbitration or cross-border M&A, ensuring local lawyer participation.
- Prohibit FLCs from engaging in marketing that **implies litigation authority** or domestic legal dominance.

Cross-Border Legal Cooperation Frameworks

Indonesia can position itself as a **leader in ASEAN legal integration** by:

- Signing **mutual recognition agreements (MRAs)** on legal services with partner countries.
- Participating in ASEAN forums for **legal education exchange**, internship mobility, and comparative research.
- Promoting Indonesian law and jurisdiction as an **arbitration-friendly** environment to attract global dispute resolution.

Safeguards and Sanctions

A comprehensive FLC policy must include:

- **Clear penalties** for unauthorized practice of law, including deportation and permit revocation.
- Disciplinary oversight involving **PERADI ethics committees**, even for foreign affiliates.

- Firm-level accountability for any FLC misconduct or breach of Indonesian regulations.

Embracing Innovation in Legal Services

Finally, reform should address technological globalization:

- Regulate **virtual foreign legal consulting** by including provisions for cross-border video consultation and online service licensing.
- Require **data protection compliance** and territorial legal disclaimers for international firms.
- Monitor AI-based legal platforms offering foreign legal services in Indonesia to **prevent unauthorized practice of law**.

Conclusion:

Indonesia has a unique opportunity to craft a regulatory framework that both **welcomes global legal collaboration** and **fortifies the nation's legal identity**. With clear, enforceable, and forward-thinking policy reforms, foreign lawyers can serve as contributors—not competitors—in Indonesia's legal future.

Conclusion

Navigating the Future of Foreign Legal Practice in Indonesia

The intersection between **global legal collaboration** and **Indonesia's legal sovereignty** presents a dynamic yet delicate challenge. As this book has explored, Indonesia—like many nations—is under increasing pressure to adapt to the demands of **international legal cooperation** while protecting the **integrity of its legal profession**.

Through an overview of existing laws, case studies, comparative practices, and policy directions, we arrive at a central conclusion: **Indonesia does not need to choose between openness and protection—it must instead strike a thoughtful balance**.

Key Takeaways:

- The role of foreign lawyers in Indonesia is clearly limited to **non-Indonesian legal advisory services**, under the title of **Foreign Legal Consultant** (FLC).
- These restrictions are grounded in national legal identity, public interest, and professional sovereignty—not in isolationism.
- International practices—from ASEAN to Europe and North America—show a shared caution in permitting foreign participation in domestic law.
- The way forward lies in **codifying transparent rules**, **strengthening collaboration**, and ensuring **mutual benefit** for both foreign consultants and Indonesian legal professionals.

Vision Forward:

Indonesia has the capacity to become a **regional leader in legal modernization**—not just in economic law but in establishing a model of **controlled, ethical, and collaborative foreign lawyer integration**. By setting clear boundaries and encouraging cooperation, Indonesia will:

- Build a more **competitive legal services market**,
- Ensure **professional knowledge exchange**, and
- Reinforce its commitment to **sovereignty in the rule of law**.

Final Thought:

Foreign lawyers are not the future of Indonesia's legal system. But they can, under the right framework, be **valuable contributors to its global presence, competitiveness, and legal diplomacy**. The key lies in regulation—not rejection; in cooperation—not compromise.

Appendices

Supporting Documents & References

This section provides supplementary materials referenced throughout the book to enhance understanding, allow further research, and offer readers access to **primary legal sources** and **policy instruments** relevant to foreign legal practice in Indonesia.

Appendix A: Key Legal Instruments in Indonesia

1. **Law No. 18 of 2003** on Advocates (UU Advokat)
2. **Government Regulation No. 2 of 2008** on Requirements and Procedures for Acquiring License to Practice Law
3. **Regulation of the Minister of Law and Human Rights No. 26 of 2017** on the Requirements and Procedures for the Appointment of Foreign Legal Consultants
4. **PERADI Code of Ethics**
5. **Ministerial Circular Letter (SEMA) No. B-3473/PW.01/10/2017** – Clarification on FLC Practices
6. **Indonesia Investment Coordinating Board (BKPM) Guidelines** – Legal service sectors in foreign investment
7. **Relevant decisions from Indonesia's Constitutional Court** concerning legal professional access and foreign participation

Appendix B: ASEAN Legal Practice Guidelines

1. **ASEAN Framework Agreement on Services (AFAS)** – Legal Services Sector
2. **ASEAN Mutual Recognition Arrangement (MRA)** – Legal professional discussions
3. **ASEAN Law Association (ALA)** regional reports on cross-border legal services

Appendix C: Sample FLC Licensing Requirements (Indonesia)

- Proof of five years of relevant legal practice experience
- Legal degree from a recognized university
- Recommendation letter from a bar association or relevant authority in the country of origin
- Curriculum Vitae (CV) and professional portfolio
- Affiliation agreement with an Indonesian law firm
- Statement of willingness not to engage in Indonesian legal proceedings or court representation
- Valid residence and work permit in Indonesia
- Sworn declaration of compliance with Indonesian laws and regulations

Bibliography

Cited Laws, Regulations, Articles, and Research

This bibliography includes all **primary legal texts**, **government regulations**, **academic references**, and **official policy documents** consulted or cited throughout this book. It aims to support further reading and legal research, especially for lawyers, academics, policymakers, and foreign legal professionals interested in the Indonesian legal framework.

Indonesian Legal References

- Law No. 18 of 2003 on Advocates (Undang-Undang Advokat)
- Law No. 25 of 2007 on Investment
- Government Regulation No. 2 of 2008 on Practice Licensing
- Minister of Law and Human Rights Regulation No. 26 of 2017 on Foreign Legal Consultants
- Ministerial Circular Letter No. B-3473/PW.01/10/2017
- The Indonesian Civil Code (Kitab Undang-Undang Hukum Perdata)
- The Indonesian Criminal Code (Kitab Undang-Undang Hukum Pidana)
- PERADI Code of Ethics
- Legal Aid Law No. 16 of 2011
- Constitutional Court Decisions relevant to legal practice and foreign involvement

ASEAN & International References

- ASEAN Framework Agreement on Services (AFAS) – Legal Sector Annex
- ASEAN Law Association Reports on Regional Legal Integration
- The International Bar Association (IBA) Guidelines on Cross-Border Legal Practice
- WTO Guidelines on Trade in Legal Services (General Agreement on Trade in Services - GATS)
- UNCITRAL Model Law on Cross-Border Insolvency
- Legal Profession Acts and Bar Council guidelines (Singapore, Malaysia, UK, USA, Japan, Australia)

Academic & Professional Sources

- Lindsey, Tim. ***Indonesia: Law and Society***. Federation Press, 2021.
- Bedner, Adriaan. ***Administrative Courts and Legal Culture in Indonesia***. BRILL, 2001.
- Pompe, Sebastiaan. ***The Indonesian Supreme Court: A Study of Institutional Collapse***. Cornell SEAP, 2005.
- Mariotti, Chiara. "Legal Pluralism and Foreign Participation in Southeast Asia." ***Asian Journal of Law and Society***, 2020.
- PERADI official publications and national conference materials
- Legal policy analysis from ***Hukumonline.com***, ***Kompasiana.com***, and academic blogs
- Interviews with Indonesian legal practitioners and law firm partners (2024–2025)

About the Author

Muhammad Ari Pratomo

Indonesian Lawyer, Author, Musician, and Legal Podcaster

Muhammad Ari Pratomo—widely recognized under the professional name **MuhammadAriLaw**—is an Indonesian lawyer whose work bridges **law, public communication, and cultural advocacy**. With a strong belief that law should be understandable, accessible, and empowering for all, he has dedicated his career to both **legal education** and **policy innovation**.

Ari is known for making complex legal topics **digestible and relevant** through his writings, music, and social media engagement. His public persona blends legal professionalism with creative expression—earning him respect as both a **scholar-practitioner** and a voice for **justice reform** in Indonesia.

He holds a formal legal background and has been involved in cross-border legal discussions, human rights advocacy, and initiatives promoting Indonesia's legal modernization. Ari is also the author of several published works, a host of the MuhammadAriLaw Podcast, and an advocate for the ethical regulation of foreign legal consultants in Indonesia.

Beyond law, he writes fiction and poetry, composes music, and actively speaks on platforms about the evolving intersection of **law, media, and human values**.

"I believe the law is not just about rules, but about restoring voice, dignity, and justice for those who have been silenced."

Don't miss out!

Visit the website below and you can sign up to receive emails whenever Muhammad Ari Pratomo publishes a new book. There's no charge and no obligation.

https://books2read.com/r/B-A-YQCSD-MRMOG

BOOKS 2 READ

Connecting independent readers to independent writers.

Also by Muhammad Ari Pratomo

LEGAL MECHANISMS OF FOREIGN INVESTMENT iN NDONESIA
The Daily Pen of a Lawyer
Foreign Lawyers in Indonesia: Between Global Collaboration and Legal Sovereignty
The Final Judgement
Youth at the End of Time – A Guide to a Broken World
Back to Father's Embrace

Watch for more at https://muhammadarilaw.com.

About the Author

Author ProfileName: Muhammad Ari PratomoOccupation: Lawyer, Writer, SongwriterBorn: Indonesia, June 21, 1982Instagram: @MuhammadAriLawTikTok: @MuhammadAriLawYouTube: @MuhammadAriLawLinkedIn: Muhammad Ari PratomoX (Twitter): @MuhammadAriLaw

Read more at https://muhammadarilaw.com.

About the Publisher

PT MuhammadAriLaw Pustaka Nada

is a book publisher based in Indonesia, founded by Muhammad Ari Pratomo—a lawyer, writer, and songwriter. The publisher is dedicated to works that voice justice, awaken empathy, and weave the power of law, literature, and conscience into a global literary movement.

Read more at https://mpnpublishing.com.

www.ingramcontent.com/pod-product-compliance
Lightning Source LLC
LaVergne TN
LVHW090433210926
848480LV00002B/810

* 9 7 9 8 2 3 1 7 8 1 4 8 5 *